Native Recipes

Gifts from the Grandmothers

By John Wisdomkeeper

Amazon Print ISBN **9781772990393**

A quality publisher of genre fiction.
Airdrie Alberta

Copyright by John Makowski 2012
Cover art Michelle Lee
Artist Mike Brodie

Acknowledgement

Recipes shared by grandmothers from many cultures both Natives and non-Natives during my travels on the Red Road. Special recognition to Lillian Mack a very special Grandmother who has gone to the spirit world but who spent many hours updating these recipes with ingredients and methods that would work in modern kitchens.

Illustration by Mike Brodie

NATIVE RECIPES

NATIVE RECIPES	5
FAMILY FEASTS	9
Soups and Stews	11
Buffalo Oven Stew	11
Biscuit Topping	12
Basic Brown Stock	13
Squamish Corn Soup	14
Curried Squash Soup	15
Pea Soup With Wild Rice	16
Pheasant Soup	17
Roundhouse Pea Soup	18
Moosejaw Chili	19
Shuswap Corn Chowder	20
Klahowya Clam Chowder	21
Wild Vegetable Cream Soup	22
Basic Bean Soup	23
Elk and Barley Soup	24
Breads, Rolls and Preserves	25
Indian Fry Bread	25
Pumpkin Loaves	26
Sourdough Starter	27
White Sourdough Bread or Rolls	28
Rose hip Jam	30
Chokecherry Jelly	30
Dandelion Sun Fritters	31
Campfire Bannock	32
Indian Harvest Bread	33
Molasses Bread	34
Bush Biscuits	35
Apple Bread	36
Salads and Appetizers	38
Blueberry Salad	38
Cat n' Fiddle Salad	39
Carrot Molded Salad	40
Bean and Egg Salad	41
Warm Cucumber Beet Salad	42

Wild Cranberry Salad	43
Cranberry Pineapple Salad	44
Cabbage Slaw	45
Jelled Beet Salad	46
Jellied Cran-Apple Salad	47
Wild Ginger Carrot Salad	48
Rainbow Pea Bean Salad	49
Strawberry wild Rice Salad	50
Snappy Shrimp Salad	51
Wahuwapa Balls	52
Wild Meat Kabobs	53
Salmon Spread	54
Beef or Venison Jerky	55
Meat and Vegetable Dishes	56
Venison or Moose Cabbage Rolls	56
Herbed Rice for Wild Game Casserole	58
Wild Game Casserole	59
Creamed Cabbage	60
Baked Game Hen	61
Oven Fried Pork Chops	62
Spicy Beer Ribs	63
Roast Tom Turkey	64
Chicken Fried Steak	65
Mashed squash	66
Anasazi Dried Beans	67
Stir Fried Trout with Dandelion Greens	68
Elk Tenderloin Brandy Mustard Sauce	69
Snappy Catfish	70
Corny Turnip Casserole	71
Indian Trail Beans	72
Hot Spiced Ribs	73
Golden Chicken Delight	74
Bear Meat Loaf	75
Sweet Potatoes Stuffed With Cranberries	76
Stuffed Roast Pork Tenderloin	77
Sweet Potato Harvest	78
Salmon and Roast Garlic	79
Roast Duck with Apricots	80
Whole Roasted Salmon	81

Pickled Carrots	82
Roast Loin of Venison with Cranberries	83
Papoose Balls	85
Roast Wild Duck	86
Desserts	87
Bluejay Feast Cake	87
Berry Whip	87
Lemony Marrow Pie	89
Spicy Rhubarb Cake	90
Syrupy Apple Cobbler	91
Elegant Blueberry Cake	92
Strawberry Shortcake	93
Mishimini Cheese Cake	94
Rhubarb Berry Cake	95
MOTHER EARTH'S PLANT WORLD	96
Remedies To Make With Dried Herbs	96
Teas	97
Infusions	97
Decoctions	98
Macerations	98
Yarrow	99
Celery	99
Dandelion	99
Wild Cherry - Dried "Bark"	100
Skull Cap	100
Sarsaparilla	100
Daisy	101
Red Clover	101
Peppermint	101
Marshmallow	102
Lady Slipper	102
Balmony	102
Wormwood	103
Iceland Moss	103
Parsley Piert	104
Horse Chestnut	104
HERBS AND THEIR USES	105
Inhalations	105
Poultices	105

Wraps	105
Liniment	105
Powders	106
Syrups	106
Baths And Washes	106

FAMILY FEASTS

It is traditional for First Nation's people to give thanks, and acknowledge our relations, to the plants, animals, birds and creatures from the water, to show respect for their giving their spirits in order for others to survive. Traditionally elders say prayers to commemorate this sacrifice at a feast gathering. During these gatherings the people shared their recipes and often demonstrated the preparation and cooking of food. Elders would pass on ancient food gathering and preparation guides to the younger members of the tribe. Because of this tradition of passing on the wisdom of the tribe from generation to generation, First Nation's people became increasingly skilled in the art of drying and preparing foods, herbs and berries with each passing generation. The Medicine men and women of the tribes were gifted healers trained by generations of ancestors in the art of using the gifts of Mother Earth to heal the people of their tribes

NOTE: Where possible recipes have been updated to include suggested modern ingredients or cooking methods. Special thanks to 94 year old Lillian Mack for her assistance in updating some of these recipes with ingredients that can be found by the modern home cook.

Soups and Stews

Buffalo Oven Stew

Two pounds of buffalo meat cut into 1 inch cubes. Note: Beef may be used if Buffalo is unavailable. Be sure to chop vegetables in uniform size so they will cook together and produce a flavourful well seasoned stew.

1 tbs. fat	1 large onion, chopped
1 1/2 tbs. salt	1 can stewed tomatoes
1 tsp. Pepper	4 carrots chopped
1/2 tsp. paprika	2 stalks of celery, chopped
1/4 cup flour	4 potatoes chopped

Fresh herbs such as basil, thyme, oregano may be added to enhance seasoning. For a spicier stew a tablespoon of salsa gives a nice zing. Brown buffalo cubes and onion in fat on high heat; reduce to simmer; mix flour, salt, pepper and paprika sprinkle over browned meat; stir and gradually add water to form gravy; Place mixture in casserole dish; add tomatoes, carrots, celery and potatoes and sufficient water to cover (leave room in the dish for the biscuit topping to be inside the rim of the dish) Place into baking dish, bake at 350 for 1 hour and 30 minutes; cover with biscuit topping and return to 425 oven for 15 minutes or until topping is golden brown.

Biscuit Topping

1 3/4 cups flour   1/4 cup shortening
4 tsp. Baking powder   1 egg
1/2 tsp. Salt   2/3 cup milk

Sift dry ingredients; cut in shortening to consistency of cornmeal; beat egg with milk; make a well in the center of dry ingredients; pour in milk mixture; stir until dough binds together; place on floured board; pat into circle, place on top of Buffalo Stew fit to edges of pan until snug; bake at 425 for 15 – 20 minutes or until top is lightly browned.

Basic Brown Stock

2 pounds beef or game (soup bones, shank, neck and ribs)
1 tbs. fat
2 quarts cold water
1 large onion, 1 carrot, 1 thin slice rutabaga
1 tbs. salt
3 whole cloves, 1 bay leaf
1/2 tsp. celery salt or celery leaves
1/4 tsp. thyme, savory or sweet marjoram

Brown meat in fat. Add cold water, cover and simmer for 1 1/2 hours. Add vegetables and seasonings and cook for 1 hour. Stain through cheesecloth, cool and remove fat before using.

Squamish Corn Soup

1/2 lb. salt pork
2 big onions, sliced
3 cups diced boiled potatoes
2 cups boiling water
2 cups cooked corn, fresh or canned
4 cups hot milk
1/2 tsp. salt, pepper to taste

Dice pork into 1/2-inch chunks, add onion, cook slowly 5-10 minutes, stirring, until transparent but not browned. Add potatoes, corn, boiling water, hot milk. Season to taste, serve with garnish. To make a thicker chowder, make a roux of 2 Tbs butter and 2 of flour, frizzled, stir this into 1 cup of the milk, cook and stir until thickened.

Curried Squash Soup

3 acorn squash, cut lengthwise and seeded
2 carrots, chopped
1 onion chopped
1 tbs. vegetable oil
1 tbs. curry powder
1 can chicken broth
1/2 cup plain yogurt
pumpkin seeds for garnish
Fill large baking dish with 1 inch of water, arrange squash cut side down, cover and steam 10-12 minutes, until tender, let cool. Saute carrots and onion in oil 10 min., add curry powder, cook 1 min. longer. Scoop pulp from squash and add to carrot mixture, add chicken broth and 1 cup water, bring to boil, reduce heat and simmer 20 minutes, put soup in bowls and swirl yogurt into soup, garnish with pumpkin seeds.

Pea Soup With Wild Rice

Soak one pound of dried peas overnight.
Precook two cups of wild rice according to package directions.
½ pound of salt pork
Carrots, turnips, sweet potato
The next morning, add three cups of water and ½ pound of salt pork to large stew pot. Add peas and bring to a boil then turn down to simmer . Chop root vegetables (about ¼ inch and all the same size for uniform cooking) Add vegetables to the stew pot and simmer covered for four hours, stir in cooked wild rice and add herbs like basil, oregano, thyme, sage. Simmer for another 15 minutes until herbs and rice are blended into soup.

Pheasant Soup

Pieces from several pheasants
1 teaspoon salt and pepper to taste
1 bay leaf
1/2 cup raw rice
1 cup raw carrots, sliced
1 small onion

Clean and wash bony pieces of pheasant well. Put in kettle with enough water to cover pieces add salt and bay leaf. Cook until meat is tender enough to fall from bones. Remove meat and bay leaf from broth. Discard bay leaf. Remove meat from bones in pieces as large as possible. Return meat and add a dash of pepper. Add uncooked rice and carrots. Cut onion in quarters and add. Simmer mixture for about one hour or until carrots and rice are tender and have soaked up most of the broth.

Roundhouse Pea Soup

1/2 cup dried split peas, 4 cups water
1 lb. Ham shank or 2 hocks
1 cup grated carrot
1 tsp. Salt
1 onion, minced
10 peppercorns, 1 bay leaf
1 cup milk
2 tbs. flour

Wash peas and soak overnight in water. Place ham shank in slow cooker, add peas and water in which they were soaked, add salt and seasonings, set to high, and allow to cook several hours. This updated version of pea soup allows for the use of a slow cooker. The recipe can also be made the traditional way by simmering 5 or 6 hours in a stew pot.

Moosejaw Chili

4 lbs. course ground lean beef/venison/moose
2 cloves garlic, minced
8 tbs. chili powder
8 tbs flour
4 tsp. salt
2 tbs. cumin
1/2 cup beef suet (may omit)
1/4 pound butter
2 cups onion, diced
2 quarts hot water
1 pint tomato puree
3 cups cooked kidney beans (optional)

Season the meat with garlic, chili powder, flour, salt and cumin, using your hands to work into meat. Heat suet and butter in heavy kettle and saute onions until soft but not brown. Stir in meat mixture and cook 20 minutes, stirring often. Add water and tomato puree. Simmer 2 hours, stirring often. If using beans stir in for the last 15 minutes.

Shuswap Corn Chowder

1/2 cup potatoes diced small	1 cup cooked corn
3 cups boiling water	½ cup celery chopped small
2 tbs. onions chopped small	1/4 cup chopped tomatoes
2 tbs. butter	
1/8 tsp. pepper	1 cup milk (or ½ and ½)

Cook potatoes in boiling water until tender; do not strain; fry onion in fat until yellow and add to potatoes; add corn, seasoning and tomatoes; cook slowly 15 minutes; add milk and bring to boiling point (do not boil)

Klahowya Clam Chowder

Clams (2 or 3 dozen) or 1 tin
1/2 cup diced salt pork
1 shallot, finely chopped
1 onion, finely chopped
1 can chicken brtoh
2 cups diced potatoes
1/2 tsp. salt
1/4 tsp. coarse ground pepper
1 lg. can tomatoes
1/2 cup diced carrots
1/4 tsp. thyme
Wash clams to remove sand; place in a pot scarcely covered with water and steam for 20 minutes; strain and remove clams from shell; combine liquor with chicken broth and set aside; braise the vegetables lightly in large pot; add the clam broth and bring to a boil; chop clams coarsely and bring to a boil with tomatoes in a separate pot; add to the vegetables; add seasonings; simmer for ten minutes

Wild Vegetable Cream Soup

1/3 cup barley
2 wild onions, diced small
2 carrots diced small
2 potatoes diced small *always chop all vegetables the same size for uniform cooking
2 leaves wild cabbage or spinach, shredded
1 tbs. butter
1 tsp. salt
1/8 tsp. pepper
4 cups milk

Cook barley in boiling water until almost tender, 30 minutes. Add vegetables and enough additional water to keep from burning. Simmer until vegetables are tender. Heat milk, add barley-vegetable mixture, butter and seasonings. Simmer 5 minutes. Do not allow milk mixture to come to a boil.

Basic Bean Soup

1 pound dried white beans (soaked overnight in lightly salted water)
6 cups chicken broth
6 cups water
2 ½ cups sliced carrots
1 ½ cups chopped onion
1 ½ cups diced celery
1 can tomatoes (drained – reserve juice)
2 tbs. olive oil
salt and pepper to taste
½ tsp. hot-pepper sauce (if desired)

Add beans, broth and water to saucepan. Boil and reduce to simmer 1 hour. Skim foam off top, add vegetables –chopped small -- carrots, onions, celery, tomatoes, reserved juice and pepper. Return to boil, reduce and cook until beans are tender (approximately one hour) stir in olive oil, salt and hot pepper sauce. Serve.

Elk and Barley Soup

1 tbs. vegetable oil
1 pound chopped elk meat (may substitute beef) cut in ½ inch cubes
2/3 cup chopped onion
6 cups beef broth
2 cups diced carrots
½ cup barley
1 tsp. dried thyme
12 tsp. salt
1 pound fresh Kale (steamed and chopped) or 1 package frozen (may substitute spinach)
8 oz. Mushrooms (sliced)

Heat oil in skillet, add beef and onion and cook stirring occasionally, until meat is well browned. Add broth, carrots, barley, thyme and salt. Bring to a boil, reduce heat, cover and simmer 1 hour, add kale and mushrooms, return to a boil, reduce heat and cover. Simmer 5 to 10 minutes longer until vegetables are tender.

Breads, Rolls and Preserves

Indian Fry Bread

2 cups flour
1 tsp. salt
2 tsp. baking powder
1/2 cup dried milk
1 tsp. sugar (optional)
1 cup warm water (or warm milk)
Mix ingredients and knead lightly, then pat out in 8" x 10" circles on floured board to ½ inch thick. Cut into pie-shaped wedges. Cut small slit in the center of each. Fry in hot fat until nicely browned. (Don't over-knead dough or bread will be tough) Garnish with a mixture of cinnamon and sugar – or jam or savory as desired

Pumpkin Loaves

3 cups flour
½ tsp. salt
½ tsp. baking powder
1 tsp. baking soda
1 tsp. ground cloves
1 tsp. ground cinnamon
1 tsp. ground nutmeg
2 cups sugar
3/4 cup butter or margarine (softened)
2 eggs
1 cup pumpkin

Sift flour and salt, add baking power, soda and spices; set aside; in large bowl of mixer beat sugar with butter until blended; add eggs, one at a time, beating well after each, continue beating until light and fluffy; beat in pumpkin at very low speed add flour mixture; mix until combined and smooth; turn into lightly greased loaf pans (2); bake 1 hour and 15 minutes or until tested done.

Sourdough Starter

2 cups warm water into container
1 pkg. Active yeast
1 level tbs. dried yeast
1 cup white flour
Mix ingredients to form smooth paste, cover loosely with lid, place container in warm place, leave for 24 hours. Sourdough starter can be kept in refrigerator for several weeks. Each time you use starter, pour off 1 cup of starter and set it aside as a starter for the next baking. Replenish by adding flour and warm water, nothing else. The mixture improves with time and once fermentation is under way, this cup of starter will be sufficient to sour the flour overnight.

White Sourdough Bread or Rolls

Put 1 cup of starter into mixing bowl
Add 2 1/2 cup of flour and stir lightly
Add 2 cup warm water
Mix thoroughly. Cover with plastic wrap.
Place in warm spot overnight (12 hours)
In the morning add:
1 cup water – warm
1 pkg. Yeast (1 tbs.)
1/2 tbsp. Sugar
2 tbs. butter
1 1/2tbs. sugar
2 tsp. Salt
4 cup white flour
1/4 tsp. Baking soda

Add yeast and sugar to warm water; still until yeast is broken down. Add to starter in your mixing bowl; liquid alternating with flour, stirring and adding until too stiff to mix with spoon. Turn out on floured board, kneading with hands, and adding more flour if needed to make soft dough. Briefly knead dough. Place kneaded dough in greased mixing bowl; cover with plastic wrap, and let rise until double in bulk. Knead briefly, divide dough into pieces to fill bread pans, fold into the shape of a loaf, place in warm greased pans, brush with melted butter, put in warm place, and let rise until double in bulk. Preheat oven to 425, bake loaves for 5 min. Reduce oven to 350 and bake for 20 to 25 min. Until bread is loose on sides of pans. For rolls follow above steps, but add 1 tbs. shortening and 1 tbs. sugar and shape into rolls and place on greased baking pan. Bake for 20 min. at 400 degrees

Rose hip Jam

2 cups rose hips, fully ripe (best after touched with frost)
4 cups boiling water
2 pounds sugar
¾ pound cooking apples
Wash hips add to boiling water, boil gently until soft. Mash, strain through a jelly bag, drip overnight. Measure juice, make up to 3 cups with water if necessary. Cook apples, rub through sieve. Mix juice and pulp, bring to a boil. Add sugar stir to dissolve, boil to jelly stage. Pour into sterilized jars and seal

Chokecherry Jelly

1 pound stoned chokecherries
to 3/4 pound sugar.
Stone cherries, mince
combine with sugar,
Let stand 2 to 3 hours, cook slowly, stirring frequently until thick. Pour into sterilized jelly glasses and seal.

Dandelion Sun Fritters

1 ½ cups whole wheat flour
2 tsp. baking powder
1 tsp. salt
1 tbs. melted butter or oil
1 egg (beaten)
1 tbs. sugar
½ cup flour
2 tbs. powdered milk
Pinch of salt
2 cups dandelion blossoms
Mix dry ingredients; add milk, egg and butter. Mix well, add blossoms which have been rinsed under cold water. Drop by spoonfuls onto greased griddle and fry until golden brown. Fold ingredients into flour mixture; bake 1 hour at 350. Test for doneness. Let sit 10 min. before removing from pan.

Campfire Bannock

5 cups flour (all purpose)
5 tsp baking powder
1 Tbs salt
1/2-3/4 cup shortening (lard)
Water

Mix all dry ingredients together. Cut in lard. Add water--enough that the dough holds together well, but not so much that the dough becomes sticky (if it sticks to your fingers-- add more flour). Once the dough is thoroughly mixed place on a greased baking sheet and pat down to about 1 inch in thickness. Bake at about 400-450F until the Bannock appears to be slightly brown. This recipe is also suitable for deep frying, frying, and pan cooking. To bake over a campfire. Divide the dough into palm sized balls. Shape each ball to about eight inches by rolling between hands. Wrap each dough length around a stick and bake over a bed of red-hot coals. Turn frequently to bake evenly.

Indian Harvest Bread

1 1/3 cup corn meal
2 quarts boiling water
2 tsp. salt
1 1/3 tsp. cinnamon
1 tsp. cloves
3 1/3 cups evaporated milk
1 cup molasses
2 cups sugar
1 cup raisins

Stir corn meal into boiling salted water and cook slowly for 10 minutes; stirring constantly; add other ingredients, mix well and cook in a double boiler 45 to 50 minutes.

Molasses Bread

2 cups Molasses
½ cup honey
2 cups wheat flour
1/2 cup white flour
1 tsp. cinnamon
1/2 tsp. salt
2 tsp. baking powder
2 eggs
1 cup oil
Combine dry ingredients and form a well in center. Add liquids and mix until smooth. Pour into loaf pan and bake in 350 oven for 30 minutes, or until toothpick inserted into center comes out clean.

Bush Biscuits

2 cups flour
1 tbs. baking powder
1 tsp. salt
1/3 cup shortening
¾ cup milk

Combine dry ingredients, cut in shortening with a fork or pastry cutter until crumbly. Add milk, mix with dry ingredients until they form a batter. Drop dough from a tablespoon onto a greased baking sheet. Bake in 450 oven for 10 to 12 minutes until lightly browned. To make smooth, rolled biscuits, increase flour until stiffer dough is formed, place dough on flour- covered surface and roll to approximately ½ inch thickness. Cut with large glass or biscuit cutter and bake as for drop biscuits.

Apple Bread

2 cups flour
¾ cup sugar
½ tsp. salt
1 pkg. dry yeast
½ cup milk
¼ cup butter
1 egg
½ cup pared and sliced apples
½ tsp. cinnamon
2 tbs. melted butter

Combine flour, ¼ cup of the sugar, salt and yeast in mixing bowl. Heat milk and butter over low heat, and add to flour mixture. Beat 2 minutes at medium speed. Add egg and ¼ cup flour. Beat 2 minutes at high speed. Stir in enough remaining flour to make a soft dough. Turn out on lightly floured board and knead until dough is smooth and elastic (about 5 minutes). Place in greased bowl, turning dough over to grease on all sides. Let rise until double in bulk (about 1 hour). Punch down and cover. Let rest 10 minutes. Pat out dough to fill bottom of greased 9 inch square pan. Arrange apples on top of dough. Combine remaining 1/2 cup sugar and cinnamon and sprinkle over apples. Drizzle melted butter over the top. Cover and let rise in warm place until doubled (about 30 minutes). Bake 40 minutes in 350 oven.

Salads and Appetizers

Blueberry Salad

2 sm. pkgs. grape gelatin
2 cups boiling water
1 large can crushed pineapple (with juice)
1 pint blueberries
1 8oz pkg. cream cheese
½ pint sour cream
½ cup sugar
4 tsps. vanilla
chopped pecans
Dissolve gelatin in boiling water add pineapple with juice; add blueberries and chill until firm Topping: combine cream cheese, sour cream, sugar and vanilla, mix well; spread over firm gelatin; sprinkle with pecans. (*updated recipe to suit modern ingredients)

Cat n' Fiddle Salad

3 cups Fiddle Head Ferns Be Sure They Are Not Unrolled (Open)
1 cup leeks
1 cup Of cattail shoots (young
2 cups of lettuce
sunflower seeds to taste
½ cup Olive oil
wild garlic *may substitute regular garlic
Pick the fiddlehead when they are up to 6 inches in height and unopened wash these and then drain. Chop leeks add to the fiddlehead. Pick cattails early in the spring also and peel first layer to get to the tender shoots, the roots are also used as well wash and chop and then drain. Cut up some lettuce and add to the others. Add sunflower seeds. Then add some oil and salt and pepper, a little wild garlic is the best or regular garlic.

Carrot Molded Salad

1 pkg. Lemon gelatin
1 cup boiling water
1 cup pineapple yogurt
1 cup grated carrots
1 tsp. lemon juice
Dissolve gelatin in boiling water and chill until slightly thickened. Fold in yogurt, carrots and lemon juice. Pour into mold and chill until firm. (*modernized to suit modern ingredients)

Bean and Egg Salad

1/2 cup mayonnaise
1 tbs. prepared mustard
1 medium onion
1 cup sliced celery
1 small cucumber
2 cans red kidney beans
4 hard boiled eggs
Seasoned salt to taste

Mix mayonnaise, mustard, onion, celery and cucumber. Fold in drained beans and eggs (cut in 1/3 chunks). Sprinkle with seasoning salt. Chill 2 to 3 hours.

Warm Cucumber Beet Salad

2 cucumbers, partially peeled and cut into ¼ inch slices
1 shallot, sliced
2 tbs. fresh or tsp. dried dill
½ tsp. sugar
¼ tsp. salt
2 tbs. vegetable oil
2 tbs. white wine vinegar
1 small head chicory
1 16 oz. can drained whole beets
Saute cucumber, shallot, dill, sugar and salt in oil for 3 minutes. Stir in vinegar and remove from heat. Place chicory on platter, arrange beets and cucumbers on platter. Pour warm dressing over salad.

Wild Cranberry Salad

2 cups ground fresh cranberries
3/4 cup sugar
3 cups miniature marshmallows (or chopped whole ones)
1/4 tsp. salt
Mix well and refrigerate overnight
The next morning add
 3 cups diced apples
1/2 cup walnuts
1/2 pint whipping cream (whipped until stiff) (or 2 cups of whipped topping) Fold into cranberry mixture and chill until ready to serve.

Cranberry Pineapple Salad

2 boxes cherry gelatin
2 cups boiling water
1 ½ cups sugar
1 bag (1 pound) fresh cranberries
1-16 oz. can crushed pineapple
3 apples, peeled
½ cup chopped pecans

Dissolve gelatin in hot water and add sugar. Grind cranberries and apples (chop fine in food processor). Add gelatin and remaining ingredients. Chill overnight.

Cabbage Slaw

¾ cup mayonnaise
2 tbs. soy sauce
2 tbs. vinegar
2 tsp. sugar
1 tsp. salt
1 cabbage shredded very fine
1-6 oz. can water chestnuts (drained and sliced)
1-6 oz. can bamboo shoots (drained and diced)
2 tbsp. chopped pimento
½ cup green onions chopped
Toss and Chill.

Jelled Beet Salad

1 pkg. Strawberry gelatin
1 pkg. Raspberry gelatin
1 pkg. Cherry gelatin
1 sm. can pineapple chunks
1 small can shredded beets
1 cup mayonnaise
½ cup chopped celery
¼ cup chopped onion

Dissolve gelatin with 3 cups water; add pineapple and beets. Chill until set. Combine mayonnaise, celery and onion and spread over chilled gelatin.

Jellied Cran-Apple Salad

2 cans whole berry cranberry sauce
2 cups boiling water
2 pkgs. Strawberry gelatin
2 tbs. lemon juice
½ tsp. salt
1 cup mayonnaise
2 cups diced apple
½ cup chopped walnuts

Melt cranberry sauce over medium heat. Drain, and mix cranberry liquid with water and gelatin, stir until dissolved. Add lemon juice and salt. Chill until mixture mounds on spoon. Add mayonnaise, beat until smooth, fold in cranberries, apple and nuts. Pour into 2 quart mold. Chill overnight.

Wild Ginger Carrot Salad

2 cups sliced cooked carrots
2 cups sliced celery
1 cup sugar
¼ cup finely diced preserved ginger
1 ½ cups white vinegar
Drain liquid from carrots (reserve liquid), combine carrots and celery in medium size bowl, stir sugar, ginger and vinegar into carrot liquid. Heat, stirring constantly to boiling. Cook rapidly about 15 minutes until medium syrup is formed. Pour syrup over carrot mixture, mix and chill overnight.

Rainbow Pea Bean Salad

1 can green beans
1 can wax beans
1 can red kidney beans
1 can chick peas
1 can lima beans
Recipe has been updated to use cans – 16 oz – home cooked vegetables and soaked and cooked dried beans and peas will produce a superior flavor
½ cup vegetable oil
¾ cup sugar
½ cup vinegar
Salt and pepper to taste
Drain beans and combine in medium bowl. Mix together oil, sugar, vinegar, salt and pepper; pour over beans and stir. Refrigerate several hours.

Strawberry wild Rice Salad

½ cup rice
3 cups water
1 pkg. Wild strawberry gelatin
½ cup sugar
1 small can crushed pineapple
Whipped topping
Cook rice in water until tender, drain, reserve water. Dissolve gelatin in 1/2 cup hot rice water. Add sugar, rice and pineapple. Refrigerate until partly set, add whipped cream or topping as desired. chill. Garnish with whole strawberries and serve.

Snappy Shrimp Salad

1 cup mayonnaise
1/4 cup Thousand Island dressing
1/4 cup chili sauce
1 tsp. prepared horseradish
1 tsp. Worcestershire sauce
1 1/2 tsp. salt
1/2 tsp. Tabasco sauce
1 lb. cooked, cleaned shrimp
Shredded lettuce

Combine ingredients, mix well and serve over the shredded lettuce.

Wahuwapa Balls

Ground Dried Corn Kernels
Dried Chokecherry or Saskatoons
Lard (or substitute water)
Grind dried flour corn kernels in a hand grinder. Grind dried Chokecherry or Saskatoons. Mix the corn and berries together at a ratio of 4 corn to 1 berry. Put lard in a frying pan and lightly brown the mixture.

Wild Meat Kabobs

2 lbs any wild game meat cut in cubes
2 tbs. Worcestershire sauce
¼ cup lime or lemon juice
1 tsp. onion powder
1 tsp. garlic powder
1 tsp. seasoning salt
1 bay leaf
¼ cup olive oil

Mix together all ingredients (except meat) pour over meat cubes and marinate overnight. Prepare bite size chunks of green/red peppers; tomato; mushrooms; onions; pineapple brush skewers with oil; alternate meat cubes with vegetable chunks on skewer; arrange on rack in oven and broil 3 to 5 min. turn and broil 2 to 3 min. Serve with hot pepper sauce or teriyaki.

NOTE: To get rid of the gamey taste of wild meat soak overnight in buttermilk, in the morning discard buttermilk and follow recipe.

Salmon Spread

2 envelops unflavored gelatin
½ cup water
1 can (16 oz) salmon
1 cup chopped onion
½ cup mayonnaise
½ cup sour cream
2 tbs. lemon juice
½ tsp. garlic salt
¼ tsp. dill weed
¼ tsp. pepper
4 sprigs parsley
Soften gelatin in water; dissolve over hot water; place remaining ingredients in blender; blend until smooth; mix in gelatin; pour into 5 cup mold; chill until firm; garnish with parsley, pimento and sliced green onion; serve with assorted crackers

Beef or Venison Jerky

8 lb Venison/beef roast
1 tbs. Salt
¼ tsp. Black pepper
1 tsp. White pepper
½ tsp. Red pepper
1 tsp.p. Meat tenderizer
2 tbs. Seasoned salt
2 tsp. Accent
1 tsp. Garlic powder
1 tbs. Kitchen bouquet
2 tbs. Morton tender quick
1/3 c Worcestershire sauce
1/3 c Soy sauce
1/3 c Barbecue sauce

Cut meat in thin slices. Combine salt, pepper, seasoning and meat tenderizers, add kitchen bouquet, Morton tender quick, Worcestershire sauce, soy sauce, barbecue sauce and liquid smoke. Marinate meat in sauce for 24 hours in a plastic freezer bag. Place meat directly on oven racks, line bottom of oven with foil and dry in oven for 6-8 hours on lowest setting.

Meat and Vegetable Dishes

Venison or Moose Cabbage Rolls

12 large cabbage leaves
1 tsp. olive oil
1 1/2 lb. Ground meat (may substitute ground beef)
4 tbs. grated onion
1/2 cup butter
1 1/2 cup cooked rice
2 tbs. chopped dill
3 cans tomato sauce
1 tbs. Worchestershire sauce
salt and pepper to taste

NOTE: To get rid of the gamey taste of wild meat soak overnight in buttermilk, in the morning discard buttermilk and follow recipe.

Brown meat and onion in butter, drain fat, mix in rice, dill, salt and pepper, Worchestershire. Core cabbage, steam until soft and easily removed, place mound of meat mixture in the center of each leaf, secure with a toothpick and place in lightly oiled baking dish, pour sauce over cabbage rolls, cover and bake 45 min. in 325 oven. Flavor is superior with wild meat, but recipe has been updated to accommodate modern ingredients

Herbed Rice for Wild Game Casserole

2 tbs. butter
1 green onion, chopped
¼ cup chopped parsley, ¼ tsp. Thyme, ¼ tsp. sage *
salt and pepper to taste
1 cup brown rice
2 ½ cups water
½ tsp. garlic powder
Saute green onion in butter until golden; add seasonings, salt and pepper, add rice and pour water over rice; boil until liquid is absorbed; transfer to covered baking dish and sprinkle with paprika. Bake 20 minutes.
*if available substitute fresh herbs

Wild Game Casserole

1 onion chopped
6 oz. Extra sharp grated cheese
1 can cream of chicken soup, 1 can mushroom soup
2 cups cooked rice
¼ cup slivered and browned almonds
1 ½ lbs. ground meat (wild or beef)
1 can mushroom buttons and juice
1 cup shredded cabbage and green pepper
Brown onion, add meat, brown and drain grease, salt lightly, add remaining ingredients, and bake in casserole dish at 350 for 30 minutes. Serve with Herbed Rice

Creamed Cabbage

1 cup milk
3 cups shredded cabbage
½ cup half and half
3 tbs. butter
3 tbs. flour
salt and pepper to taste
Scald milk, add cabbage and cook 3 minutes; blend flour and half and half, add butter and slowly add to cabbage, cook 2 minutes longer, stirring constantly, add seasonings and serve.

Baked Game Hen

1 Game Hen
¼ cup flour
½ tsp. salt, 1/4 tsp. pepper
¼ tsp seasoning salt
Dash thyme and basil
Slice bacon and 1 chicken heart
¼ cup melted butter
½ cup milk

Mix seasonings with flour, dredge game hen and bacon. Roll bacon around chicken heart, fasten with toothpick and insert in cavity of game hen. Brown hen in melted butter in skillet. Transfer to baking dish and bake 1 hour in 325 oven. Remove hen, sprinkle 2 tbs. flour in baking dish, place on burner at medium, mix flour with drippings, gradually stir in milk, bring to boil, stirring constantly until smooth for gravy.

Oven Fried Pork Chops

3 tbs. butter
1 egg beaten
2 tbs. milk
1 cup of corn meal stuffing (may use packaged)
4 pork chops
Melt butter in baking pan; mix egg and milk, dip pork chops in egg mixture; coat with stuffing mix, place chops in pan. Bake 20 minutes; turn and bake 10 to 15 minutes longer.

Spicy Beer Ribs

4 pounds spareribs
1 can beer
½ cup dark corn syrup
1/3 cup vegetable oil
½ cup chopped onion
1/3 cup mustard
1 to 2 tbs. chili powder
2 cloves garlic

Mix beer, corny syrup, onion, mustard, vegetable oil, chili powder and garlic; pour into plastic bag and add ribs to bag. Close bag and marinate ribs in mixture overnight. Remove ribs from marinade; place in shallow baking pan and bake in 350 oven 40 to 45 minutes, basting frequently with marinade. For excellent barbecued ribs, remove from oven and place on hot grill (6 inches) from heat until crisp brown on both sides.

Roast Tom Turkey

One good sized turkey
salt and pepper
2 tbs. melted butter or margarine
giblets
1 onion
1 celery stick
1 tsp. poultry seasoning (sage)
dried bread cubes (or box of stuffing mix)

Rinse turkey, pat dry and rub salt into neck and body cavities. Melt butter in small pan, chop or slice up giblets, add to melted butter with finely chopped onion and celery, brown lightly, add water and bring giblets to a boil, reduce heat and simmer 5 or 10 minutes. Combine poultry seasoning and bread cubes in large bowl, pour giblet mixture over bread and mix lightly to moisten stuffing. Chopped nuts, raisins, mushrooms, etc may be added to stuffing at this point. Lightly fill body cavities with stuffing, tie drumsticks to turkey with string, and secure neck cavity with turkey pin or toothpick. Place in 300 oven and bake 4 to 7 hours basting frequently with liquid from turkey baking. Baking time will depend on the size of the turkey. Test for doneness by gripping drumstick.

Chicken Fried Steak

1 to 2 pounds round steak
½ pound ground sausage
2 beaten eggs
2 tbs. milk
1 cup break crumbs
Salt and pepper to taste
Fry sausage, drain fat and set aside. Pound steak with tenderizing hammer, cut into pork chop sized chunks. Stir eggs into milk, dip chunks into mixture, then roll in bread crumbs, repeat egg/crumb process, then fry in reserved sausage fat until brown on both sides. Cover and cook over low heat for 45 minutes. Prepare milk gravy with fried sausage pieces and pour over chicken fried steak before serving. Serve with homemade biscuits.

Mashed squash

1 ½ cups squash
¼ tsp mace, ¼ tsp allspice, 1 tsp ground cardamom
1 tablespoon maple syrup
½ tsp salt
2 tsp melted butter
Cut squash in half, scrape out seeds and fiber. Chunk in 2" pieces steam for 30 minutes until tender (15 minutes if using electric steamer) Cool and skin, spoon into blender, add remaining ingredients and process till smooth. Makes a wonderful squash soup

Anasazi Dried Beans

Ham end or hock
2 Cups dry beans
Water to cover
1 large onion
Garlic – to taste
Salt And pepper
Soak beans overnight; drain water and add more to cover, cook beans till nearly done keeping them covered with water the whole time. Add ham and the coarsely chopped onion and garlic and continue cooking until all the meat falls off the ham bone.

Stir Fried Trout with Dandelion Greens

6 Handfuls Of Dandelion Greens
2 Trout
Grease (may use oil) to cover bottom of cast iron fry pan (or Wok)
3 Wild Onions – or green onions
Salt and Pepper (Dash), White Sage (few pinches)
1 Lemon
Cut and clean fish. Cut into long strips. Chop onion. Slice lemon into thin disks. Wash and chop dandelion leaves. Grease cast iron fry pan slightly with bacon grease. Medium heat Add onion 5-6 thin slices of lemon, salt, pepper, and a few pinches of white sage. Let cook about 3/4 of the way and then add the dandelion leaves. Cook until leaves are soft. Add salt, pepper, sage to taste.

Elk Tenderloin with Brandy Mustard Sauce

2 elk tenderloins, 8-10 oz each
4 slices bacon
½ cup sliced mushrooms
1 tbs. hot mustard
¼ cup onion, finely diced,
¼ cup bell pepper finely diced
½ cup brown gravy
1 ½ oz. Brandy
1 clove garlic
1 tsp. Thyme

NOTE: To get rid of the gamey taste of wild meat soak overnight in buttermilk, in the morning discard buttermilk and follow recipe.

Ground black pepper to taste Remove silverskin from tenderloins and rub meat with split garlic cloves. Sprinkle lightly with thyme and black pepper. Wrap bacon around tenderloin and use toothpick to secure. Place in hot cast iron frying pan and saute until bacon is cooked. Remove from pan and pour off excess grease. Place onion and bell pepper in pan for 30 seconds, add mushrooms and saute until tender. Add brandy to hot pan and flame. When flame dies, add brown gravy and mustard and stir until mixture is smooth. Pour mixture over tenderloins on warm platter.

Snappy Catfish

¼ teaspoon garlic powder
¾ cup yellow cornmeal
4 catfish fillets - or whole catfish
¼ 4 cup flour
2 teaspoons Salt
Vegetable Oil
1 teaspoon Cayenne Pepper
Combine cornmeal, flour, salt, cayenne and garlic powder. Coat catfish with mixture, shaking off excess. Add 1" layer of oil to a large skillet. Heat to 35~. Add catfish in single layer and fry until golden brown about 4-5 minutes; drain on paper towels.

Corny Turnip Casserole

1 large turnip
Salt to taste
1 cup corn (creamed) – may use canned corn
1 tbs. sugar
Pepper to taste
1/4 tsp. Nutmeg
1/2 cup milk
Butter

Cube and boil turnip in salted water; drain and mash; add rest of ingredients; place in greased baking dish; dot with butter; sprinkle nutmeg on top and bake 1/2 hour in moderate oven.

Indian Trail Beans

1 pkg. lima or pinto beans
2 cups cooked ham, cubed
½ small onion, chopped
2 stalk celery, chopped
1 small can tomatoes
1 green and 1 red peppers
1 tsp. baking soda
salt and pepper
Soak beans in water overnight; cook in large pan with plenty of water until well done (approx. 4 hours); add ham, celery, onion, green peppers, tomatoes and baking soda; season to taste with salt and pepper; cook slowly 45 min.

Hot Spiced Ribs

One or two racks of moose or beef ribs
3 tbs. flour and 1 tsp. salt and 2 tbs. fat
1 onion chopped
¼ cup cider vinegar, 2 tbs. brown sugar
2 tbs. Worcestershire sauce, dash Tabasco sauce
1 cup water, mixed with 1/2 tsp. Dry mustard
¼ tsp. pepper and paprika mixed
½ cup diced celery

NOTE: To get rid of the gamey taste of wild meat soak overnight in buttermilk, in the morning discard buttermilk and follow recipe.

Combine flour, salt, pepper and paprika; rub into meat. Heat fat and sear the floured ribs. Lift into casserole. Add chopped onion to the fat in pan, cook and stir until golden brown; add all remaining ingredients and heat to near boiling. Pour mixture over ribs. Cover tightly and bake in 325 oven for about two hours

Golden Chicken Delight

Chicken pieces; skinned
3 eggs
1 cup milk
1/2 cup flour
1 cup bread crumbs
paprika,
salt and pepper

Line up three bowls. Whisk together egg and milk and place in first bowl. Add flour, salt, pepper and paprika to second bowl, Add bread crumbs to third bowl.
Dip chicken pieces in mixture bowl one; then dip in bowl two until coated with flour mixture. Dip back into bowl one and then dip into Bowl two, turning until coated with bread crumbs.
Fry in cast iron fry pan until golden brown on each side. Move to oven set at 350 degrees and bake 30 to 40 minutes until meat thermometer indicates 190F or 88C. If no meat thermometer is available remove thickest piece, cut into it with a knife and make sure there is no pink and chicken is fully cooked

Bear Meat Loaf

2 lb ground bear meat (may use ground beef – flavor will be slightly tamer)
1/2 cup milk
2 eggs
salt and pepper to taste
1/4 tsp. thyme
1/4 tsp. oregano
3/4 cup tomato sauce
1 cup onion, minced
1 1/2 tsp. dry mustard
1 cup bread crumbs
1/2 green pepper, finely chopped
1 small can of mushrooms or fresh mushrooms.
Mix ingredients & put in loaf pan. Bake at 350 until done (about an hour).

Sweet Potatoes Stuffed With Cranberries

1 ½ cups of cranberry sauce
3 tbs. butter
1/3 cup brown sugar
1 tsp. salt
½ cup chopped nuts
Bake potatoes until tender, peel skins and cut in half lengthwise. Scoop out insides and reserve. Stuff both halves, holding the potato back together with toothpicks. Mix sauce, nuts, sugar, butter, salt and pour over. bake at 350 uncovered until lightly browned, about 20-25 minutes

Stuffed Roast Pork Tenderloin

1 pound lean pork tenderloin
1 tablespoon all-purpose flour
3 tablespoons cornstarch
1 cup chopped onion
1/2 cup raw celery
1 clove garlic
1 bay leaf, crumbled
1 cup cooked wild rice

Trim all visible fat from pork. Split meat lengthwise, stopping about 1/2" from the edge. Open the split and flatten the meat out. Saute onions, garlic, celery and bay leaf Add 1 cup cooked wild rice and mix. Spread stuffing mixture inside the split meat. Fold meat back over itself. tie at 1" spaces with kitchen string. Bake at 350 degrees F, about an hour.

Sweet Potato Harvest

1 can sweet potatoes *or 3 or 4 whole cooked
7 tbs. butter, melted
1 apple, cored and thin sliced
¼ cup brown sugar
1 tbs. flour
¼ tsp. Cardamom
1 tbs. butter
2 tbs. chopped pecans

Mash sweet potatoes until smooth, add melted butter; in small bowl mix cold butter, brown sugar, flour and cardamom, stir in pecans and sprinkle ½ over potatoes; cover with apple slices and sprinkle remaining mixture on apples; bake for 30-40 min. until apples are crisp/tender.

Salmon and Roast Garlic

Two medium heads garlic, broken into separate cloves, peeled
1/2 cup (about) olive oil
3 tablespoons unsalted butter
Eight 6- to 7-ounce salmon fillets
4 teaspoons fresh lemon juice
4 teaspoons chopped fresh rosemary
Preheat oven to 400°F.
Place garlic in small cast iron or ovenproof dish. Pour enough oil over to cover and cover with foil
Bake garlic until very tender, about 35 minutes.
Squeeze meat out of baked garlic into blender, add 1 tablespoon cooking oil and butter to processor; puree. Season with salt and pepper.
Increase oven heat to 450. Season salmon with salt and pepper and place on baking sheet. Drizzle each fillet with ½ teaspoon lemon juice, then spread 1 tablespoon garlic puree over each. (Can be made 1 day ahead; chill.) Bake salmon uncovered until just cooked through, about 15 minutes. Sprinkle with the fresh rosemary and serve.

Roast Duck with Apricots

One 4 ½ to 5 lb. Duck
¾ tsp. salt
¾ cup dried apricots, quartered
½ cup water
1 cup sliced celery
2 tbs. butter
4 cups ½ inch bread cubes
1 tbs. sugar
¼ tsp. leaf thyme
¼ tsp. nutmeg

NOTE: To get rid of the gamey taste of wild duck soak overnight in buttermilk, in the morning discard buttermilk and follow recipe.

Wash, drain and dry duck; sprinkle salt evenly over body and neck cavities. Prepare stuffing. Combine apricots and water in saucepan; bring to boil; cover and let stand 15 min. Saute celery in butter until tender; add bread cubes, sugar, thyme and nutmeg; add apricots with liquid and mix. Fill neck and body cavities loosely with stuffing; skewer neck skin to back; cover opening of body cavity with aluminum foil and tie legs together; place on rack in shallow roasting pan; bake in a 325 oven until drumstick meat is fork tender (2 ½ to 3 hours).

Whole Roasted Salmon

1 whole salmon, about 4 lbs., cleaned
Freshly ground pepper
1 medium onion, thinly sliced
1 lemon, thinly sliced
4-5 sprigs parsley, 1 tsp. dried thyme
1 Tbs. olive oil

Preheat oven to 400 degrees F. Rinse the salmon inside out and pat it dry. Sprinkle the inside of the salmon with salt and pepper, and stuff it with half of the onion, half of the lemon, and all of the parsley. Tear off a sheet of aluminum foil large enough to wrap the salmon. Place the salmon on the foil and sprinkle with salt, pepper, and thyme. Rub with olive oil. Scatter the remaining onion and lemon slices on top and seal foil tightly. Place on a cookie sheet and bake 40-45 minutes. Cool in the foil on a rack. Remove onion and lemon; skin if desired. Serve at room temperature.

Pickled Carrots

1 pound carrots
1 tbs. mixed pickling spice
3 cups water, 1 cup cider vinegar
1 cup sugar, ½ tsp. salt
Peel carrots, cut into sticks about 4 inches long and 1/4 inch thick. Tie pickling spice in cheesecloth to make small bag. In a large saucepan bring water, vinegar, sugar, salt and spice to a boil, stirring until sugar dissolves; simmer, covered for 5 minutes. Add carrots. Simmer covered, for 2 minutes – carrots will be very crisp. Remove spice, pour carrots into a container and cover tightly. Refrigerate 2 to 3 days for flavors to blend before serving.

Roast Loin of Venison with Cranberries

2 thick slices of lemon; 2 thick slices of orange
2 slices of peeled fresh ginger
1 ½ cups sugar, 1 small bay leaf
2 cups fresh cranberries
4 pounds boneless loin of venison,
2 tablespoons olive oil, 1 tsp salt
1 ¼ teaspoons freshly ground pepper
¾ 4 teaspoon finely chopped juniper berries
2 cups dry red wine, 2 cups beef or venison stock
2 tablespoons cold butter, cut into pieces
Fresh thyme sprigs, for garnish

NOTE: To get rid of the gamey taste of wild meat soak overnight in buttermilk, in the morning discard buttermilk and follow recipe.

In a medium saucepan, combine the lemon, orange, ginger, sugar and bay leaf with 1 cup of cold water. Bring to a boil over high heat, stirring to dissolve the sugar. Reduce the heat to moderate and boil, uncovered, until syrupy, 10 to 15 minutes. Stir in the cranberries, then remove from heat and cool. Transfer the mixture to a glass container, cover and refrigerate for 1 to 2 days, stirring once or twice during that time. Preheat the oven to 400F. Rub the venison with the olive oil, ¾ teaspoon of the salt, 1 teaspoon of the pepper and ½ teaspoon of the chopped juniper berries, pressing the seasonings into the meat.

Set the loin on a rack in a roasting pan and roast, basting frequently with the pan juices, until medium-rare (about 135F on a meat thermometer), 25 to 30 minutes.

Cover the venison loosely with foil and set aside for 10 to 15 minutes before carving. Meanwhile, remove and discard the bay leaf and the lemon, orange and ginger slices from the cranberries. In a food processor or blender, puree half the cranberries and half the liquid until smooth. In a medium saucepan, boil the wine over high heat until reduced to ½ cup, about 5 minutes.

Add the stock and bring to a boil. Add the cranberry puree, reduce the heat to low and simmer, uncovered, until slightly thickened, about 10 minutes. Remove from heat. Strain the remaining whole cranberries and add them to the sauce with the remaining 1/4 teaspoon each of salt, pepper and chopped juniper berries. Swirl in the cold butter. Slice the venison thinly (stir any juices into the sauce) and serve with sauce.

Papoose Balls

1 lb. Ground venison; ½ lb. Ground pork
½ tsp. salt and dash of pepper
¼ cup cream
2 cups toasted bread cubes
4 tbs. chopped onion, 1 tbs. Parsley, 1 tsp. Poultry seasoning
1 can cream of mushroom soup and ¾ cup milk (substitute for fresh mushroom soup)
Combine meat, salt, pepper and cream, form into small patties, mix bread cubes, onion, parsley and seasoning, soften with melted place a mound of stuffing on patty, cover with second patty and form into papoose ball, sealing in stuffing, continue until all are used, brown in hot fat, transfer to baking dish, cover with soup mixed with milk, bake in 350 over 30 to 45 min.

Roast Wild Duck

1 duck
2 cups cubed dried bread
1 onion, chopped fine
¼ tsp. dill weed, ½ cup celery
1 cup diced apple
salt and pepper to taste
1 cup chicken broth
NOTE: To get rid of the gamey taste of wild meat soak overnight in buttermilk, in the morning discard buttermilk and follow recipe.

Clean duck thoroughly, soak overnight in salt water to cover. Drain off and rinse in clear water. Stuff duck and wrap tightly in heavy foil. Place in roaster and roast in slow oven 325 allowing 30 minutes per pound

Desserts

Bluejay Feast Cake

½ cup margarine
1 cup white sugar
2 eggs
¾ cup milk
2 cups flour
1 tsp baking powder
½ tsp lemon extract
½ tsp vanilla
1 cup blueberries
¾ cup brown sugar
½ tsp. cinnamon

Cream margarine and sugar, add sifted flour and dry ingredients alternately with milk; fold in blueberries; pour into 8" greased and floured pan; mix brown sugar and cinnamon, sprinkle over top; bake at 350° 35-40 minutes. Serve with berry whip topping.

Berry Whip

1 ½ cups crushed blueberries
1 cup icing sugar
2 egg whites
2 tsp. Lemon juice
pinch of salt
Combine ingredients in large bowl; beat until stiff; spread on Bluejay Feast Cake.

Lemony Marrow Pie

2 cups cooked vegetable marrow
½ tsp. Salt
½ cup white sugar
grated rind of 3 lemons
1 tbs. lemon juice
2 eggs
½ cup milk

Steam or cook marrow until tender; drain and process in blender or food processor until smooth. Add butter, salt, lemon rind and juice, beat eggs with milk add sugar and blend with marrow. Fill baked pastry shell and cook for 30 minutes in a 350 oven.

Spicy Rhubarb Cake

1 ¾ cups sifted cake flour
2 tsp. Baking powder
½ tsp. Salt ½ tsp. Soda.
1 tsp. Cinnamon, ½ tsp. Cloves
½ cup shortening
1 cup sugar
1 egg, beaten
1 cup chopped raisins
¾ cup cooked rhubarb, sweetened

Cream shortening and sugar; sift dry ingredients, add soda to rhubarb; add dry ingredients alternately with rhubarb. Bake in angel food or loaf pan at 350 degrees for 1 hour; serve with whipped cream or ice cream.

Syrupy Apple Cobbler

6 med. Apples
½ cup maple syrup
¼ cup butter or margarine
½ cup sugar
1 egg
1 cup flour
2 tsp. baking powder
½ tsp. salt
¼ cup milk

Pare and core apples; slice thin; cover with maple syrup and stir to coat; spread evenly iin greased 2 qt. Baking dish. Cream butter, add sugar, stirring constantly to cream; beat in egg. Combine dry ingredients; add alternately with milk to butter-sugar mixture; spoon over apples and smooth; bake at 400 degrees 30 minutes or until top is golden.

Elegant Blueberry Cake

2 cups miniature marshmallows
2 cups fresh blueberries
One 3 oz pkg mixed berry gelatin
2 ½ cups flour
1 cup sugar
½ cup shortening
3 tsp. baking powder
½ tsp. salt
1 cup milk
1 tsp. vanilla
3 eggs

Grease 9 x 13 baking pan. Cover bottom with marshmallows, combine blueberries and their juice with dry gelatin in separate bowl; set aside; combine remaining ingredients, beat well. Pour batter over marshmallows in pan and spoon berry-gelatin mixture over top of batter. Bake in 350 oven for 30 minutes, then reduce heat to 300 and bake 15 minutes more; Marshmallows will rise to the top and form a golden crust.

Strawberry Shortcake

½ cup melted butter
1 egg
2 cups sifted flour
2 tsp. Baking powder
1/8 tsp. Salt
Mix well and fill greased muffin tins.
2 cups chopped strawberries
sugar to sweeten
dash of lemon juice
Place muffins in dessert dishes; cover with berries and whipped cream; serve.

Mishimini Cheese Cake

Crust:
1 cup graham cracker crumbs
¼ cup melted butter
1 tbs. sugar
Filling and topping:
Two 8 oz. pkgs. cream cheese (softened)
1 ½ cups applesauce
5 tbs. sugar
3 eggs
½ tsp. grated lemon rind
1/2 cup sour cream
1 can cherry pie filling

Combine crumbs with butter and sugar; butter 8" spring form pan; press crumb mixture onto bottom and halfway up sides. Place in refrigerator to chill. Beat cheese until creamy; add 1/2 cup applesauce and beat well. Beat in four tbs. sugar; add eggs, beat well; beat in lemon rind. pour into chilled crust. Bake 45 to 50 minutes until firm; spread top with 1 cup applesauce; combine sour cream with 1 tbs. sugar and ripple through sauce; bake 5 minutes more. Cool at room temperature and then chill. Top with cherry pie filling.

Rhubarb Berry Cake

½ cup sugar
1 tsp. cinnamon
1 tbs. butter
½ cup shortening
1 ½ cups brown sugar
1 egg
1 tsp. soda
1 cup sour cream
2 cups flour
1 cup rhubarb cut in cubes
½ cup sliced strawberries
1 tsp. vanilla

Mix sugar, cinnamon and butter; set aside. Cream shortening and Brown sugar; stir in egg; combine soda and sour cream, add flour; stir in rhubarb, strawberries and vanilla. Bake in 350° over for 30 to 40 minutes

MOTHER EARTH'S GIFTS FROM THE PLANT WORLD

Remedies To Make With Dried Herbs And Their Uses

Dried plants are probably the most versatile elements used in natural remedies. Home herbal preparations are economical. Air-dried herbs lose their therapeutic properties when their active principles are destroy by heat, air, or sunlight. Dried herbs can be kept indefinitely in dark, sealed containers. Herbal preparations apply to almost any health situation. Remember if you do not have a basic knowledge of herbal remedies then you should consult a practitioner to become educated.

WARNING

The following is for informational purposes only and uses are not prescriptions or specific recommendations. A herbalist or holistic practitioner should always be consulted before endeavoring to use herbal preparations. As with any kind of medication there are many different kinds of interactions and the use and combining of herbs requires expert knowledge.

Teas

Teas are prepared by steeping the dried plant(s) in water. There are three different types of tea preparations; infusions, decoctions, and macerations.

Infusions

Prepare infusions by boiling water over plant parts, and steeping 2 minutes. When leaves are used the mixture can steep for up to 10 minutes. Infusions are prepared in a glazed enamel container, preferably covered to conserve steam. Drink infusion as soon as possible to prevent the active elements from being destroyed by heat or escaping through vapor.

Decoctions

A decoction involves placing dried plants in cold water and bringing to a boil; boil 5 minutes (10 for certain roots) in a closed container. Solution is often used for skin applications. A bouillon consists of a decoction using the whole plant, and is consumed like soup. The boiling time for bouillon varies with the species of plant. Caution over-boiling with darken and distort the herb.

Macerations

Home-made macerations involve soaking dried plants in water for days or weeks. The mixture is kept in a closed container in a cool dark place. Macerations contain high concentrations of active principles and have considerable therapeutic value. Valerian (Valeriana officinalis) roots are used as a remedy for reducing appetite.

Yarrow

Actions: Hypotensive, diuretic, hepatic, stimulant, tonic

Preparation and Dosage: Pour 1 cup boiling water onto 1-2 tsp. of dried herbs; leave to infuse for 10-15 min. drink 3 times daily

Celery

Dried ripe seeds

Actions: Anti-rheumatic, diuretic, sedative, aromatic.

Preparation and Dosage: pour cup of boiling water onto 1-2 tsp. of crushed seeds; leave to infuse 10-15 minutes; drink 3 time daily

Dandelion

Root or Leaf

Actions: Diuretic, hepatic, anti-rheumatic, laxative, tonic, blood disorders, skin eruptions, gastritis, ulcers.

Preparation and Dosage: 2-3 tsp. of root in boiling water for 10-15 min. leaves may be eaten raw in salads.

Wild Cherry - Dried "Bark"

Action: irritating coughs, bronchitis, asthma, chronic diarrhea

Preparation and Dosage: Pour a cup of boiling water onto a spoonful of dried cherries and Bark; leave to infuse for 10-15 minutes.

Skull Cap

Actions: Nervous tension, seizures, hysterical states, epilepsy, insomnia

Preparation and Dosage: 1 cup of boiling water onto 1-2 tsp. of dried herbs and leave for 10-15 min.

Sarsaparilla

Root

Actions: Arthritis, scrophula, cutaneous disease, gout conditions

Preparation and Dosage: 1-2 tsp. of root in cup of water; boil and simmer 10-15 min.

Daisy

Dried flower heads
Actions: Liver and Kidney problems, Arthritis and Rheumatism.
Preparation and Dosage: 1 tsp. of dried herb and leave to infuse for 10 min.

Red Clover

Flower heads
Actions: Childhood eczema, coughs, chronic skin eruptions
Preparation and Dosage: 1 cup boiling water onto 1-3 tsp. of herb, steep for 10-15 min.

Peppermint

Actions: Flatulence, Intestinal Colic, Nausea, Travel Sickness
Preparation and Dosage: 1 cup boiling water onto 1-2 tsp. dried herb; infuse for 10 min.

Marshmallow

Root and Leaf
Actions: Gastritis, Peptic Ulceration, Colitis, Boils, Ulcers
Preparation and Dosage: Place 2-4 grms of root into 2 - 4 cups cold water; leave to infuse overnight

Lady Slipper

Root
Actions: Sedative, hypnotic, antispasmodic, nervine tonic, analgesic
Preparation and Dosage: 1 cup of boiling water onto 1-2 tsp. of the root; let infuse for 10-15 min.

Balmony

Actions: Cholagogue, digestive and absorptive system, gal bladder, laxative
Preparation and Dosage: 1 cup boiling water and 2 tsp. dried herb. Let infuse for 10-15 minutes. Drink 3 times a day.

Wormwood

Leaves or flowering tops. Actions: Anti-inflammatory, anti-microbial, hepatic, stimulant

Preparation and Dosage: 1 cup of boiling water onto 1-2 tsp. of dried herb; leave to infuse for 10-15 min. Drink 3 times daily

Iceland Moss

Entire Plant

Actions: Anti-emetic, expectorant, anti-catarrahl, pectoral, tonic

Preparation and Dosage: 1 tsp. shredded moss in a cup of cold water; boil for 3 min.; let stand for 10 min. Drink morning and night

Parsley

Actions: kidney and urinary stones diuretic
Preparation and Dosage: pour cup of boiling water onto 1-2 tsp. of dried herb; leave to infuse 10-15 min. drink 3 times a day

Horse Chestnut

Fruit (that is the horse chestnut itself)
Actions: Astringent, circulatory tonic
Preparation and Dosage: pour 1 cup of boiling water onto 1-2 tsp. of the dried fruit and leave to infuse 10-15 min; drink 3 times daily

HERBS AND THEIR USES

Inhalations

Aromatic plants are placed in hot water so that the patient may inhale the vapours that contain the volatile active ingredients of the plant. Eucalyptus inhalations relieve sinus problems.

Poultices

Poultices combine a decoction with medicinal clay. White or green clay is used rather than gray. A poultice is applied to the skin to draw out pus. Poultices are usually applied warm but may be used cold.

Wraps

Wraps produced by soaking sterile gauze in a decoction are used to bandage ailing limbs. Sometimes the wrap is covered with a towel to conserve heat. Strains can be wrapped with a decoction of arnica leaves and flowers.

Liniment

Liniments can be made by mixing macerations with oil. Liniments are used to stimulate circulation and thus warm or cool the injured or sore area.

Powders

Dried plants can be reduced to powder with a mortar and pestle. Powders can be dusted on skin to treat external wounds. They can also be sprinkled on food or combined with water for hot or cold drinks. Blackfoot Indians applied dried powdered root of false Solomon's seal to their skin to treat boils, sores and wounds.

Syrups

Syrup can be prepared by combining an infusion or a maceration and honey and simmering to thicken. The Catawba Indians made a syrup from the boiled roots of mullein as a cough remedy for children.

Baths And Washes

Baths immerse the entire body in a preparation made from decoctions or infusions. Washes are also used locally to rinse the eyes, throat or mouth. The Delaware Indians prepared a cold infusion from purple bonnet, a wash they used for skin eruptions and irritations.

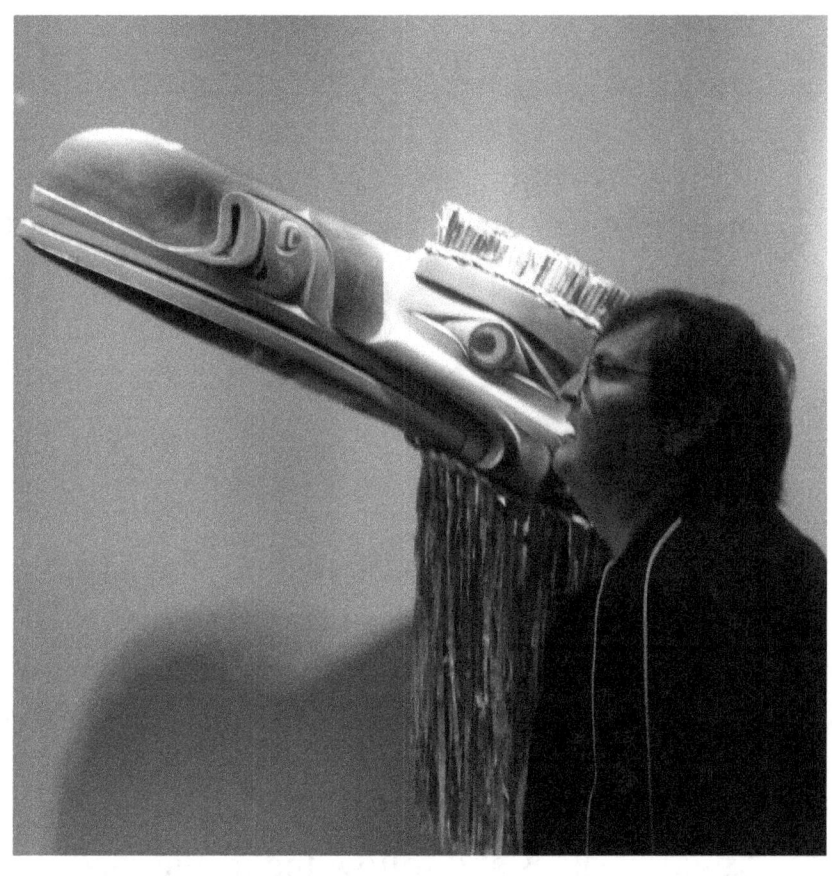

I was taken from my mother at birth and adopted by a white family. I didn't find out until I was in my teens that I was from the north country of British Columbia, descended from the Sekani Nation
The Sekani are medicine healers

Dedication

This collection is dedicated to all the travelers I met as I traveled the pathways of both the dark and the red road. This book is dedicated from my heart to the many elders who shared their spiritual experiences and who embrace their cultures in the ways they live.

My Indian name Sus' naqua ootsin' (the Wisdomkeeper) was given to me by a 100 year old lady who looked deep into my eyes and saw into my soul. My journey started on one of the Darkest Days of my life – that's when I decided to put on my red running shoes and follow the magic road.
All My Relations………

Sus' naqua ootsin'